M000303932

PRAYER PLUS
FAITH EQUALS
Miracles

31 Days of Fervent Prayer

Sharon Crittenden

Prayer Plus Faith Equals Miracles: 31 Days of Fervent Prayer

@2018 by Sharon Crittenden.

Printed in the USA

All rights reserved. No part of this book may be reproduced in any written, electronic, recording or photocopying without written permission of the author or publisher. The exception would be in the case of brief quotations embodied in the critical articles of reviews and pages where permission is specifically granted by the author or publisher.

Although every precaution has been taken to verify the accuracy of the information contained herein, the author and/or publisher assume no responsibility for any errors or omissions. No liability is assumed for damages that may result from the use of information contained within.

THE HOLY BIBLE, NEW INTERNATIONAL VERSION®, NIV® Copyright © 1973, 1978, 1984, 2011 by Biblica, Inc.® Used by permission. All rights reserved worldwide.

Italics in scripture quotations reflect the author's added emphasis.

Books may be purchased in bulk quantity by contacting the publisher directly by emailing: RhemaWordPress@gmail.com

Paperback ISBN: 978-0-692-95204-7
Ebook ISBN: 978-0-692-95202-3
*Audiobook Available January 2018

Library of Congress Catalog Number: 2017915714

Publisher's Cataloging-In-Publication Data

Names: Crittenden, Sharon.
Title: Prayer plus faith equals miracles : 31 days of fervent prayer / Sharon Crittenden.
Description: [Richton Park, Illinois] : Rhema Word Press, [2017]
Identifiers: ISBN 9780692952047 | ISBN 9780692952023 (ebook)
Subjects: LCSH: Prayer--Christianity. | Christianity--Prayers and devotions. | Faith. | Miracles.
Classification: LCC BV210.3 .C75 2017 (print) | LCC BV210.3 (ebook) | DDC 248.32--dc23

MORE WORKS FROM THE AUTHOR
Visit: www.sharoncrittenden.blogspot.com

WANT TO JOIN OUR MAILING LIST?
Send an email to: RhemaWordPress@gmail.com

CONNECT WITH THE AUTHOR

Facebook: Sharon Crittenden

Instagram
@scrittenden41

Twitter
@scrittenden42

*To submit video or written reviews email:
RhemaWordPress@gmail.com

*For bulk quantities email:
RhemaWordPress@gmail.com

"Our prayers may be awkward. Our attempts may be feeble. But since the power of prayer is in the One who hears it and not in the one who says it, our prayers do make a difference."

— **Max Lucado**

DEDICATION

This book is dedicated to my husband, Pastor Andre Crittenden who pushes me every day to be great and elevate my faith! And to everyone that desires a consistent prayer life, make time to communicate with God every day.

A portion of the proceeds from the sale of this book will be donated to organizations that foster healthy family relationships and cancer research

WHEN LIFE KNOCKS YOU DOWN, PRAY YOUR WAY UP!

Do you want to experience a fulfilling and rewarding prayer life? You won't be disappointed at what happens when you begin to put undying faith behind the words you pray! Walk the path of faith, through a simple step of obedience by praying fervently for 31 days. Commit to the challenge of communicating daily with God, and your life will transform into a miraculous journey. Enjoy what it means to commune with God as you

- o wholeheartedly discover that praying through faith is not just to get what you want out of life, but specifically for those moments when you DON'T get what you want out of life.

- o realize that tough circumstances will arise, but they are no match for the inner strength and the faith that resides inside of you!

- o consciously commit yourself to the things that produce inner strength and wake up your faith!

Living "faithless" is a self-destructive disease. In fact, prayer without faith is like a hand in a glove. You can't have one without the other. Prayer alone simply cracks open doors but hardcore faith pushes any door wide open.

Enjoy 31 days of "fervent" prayer privately or with a bible study group. However you decide, don't miss out on a chance to experience life-changing results. Journal space for extra writing of notes is included so you can reflect daily on what you have read. Share your journey with others.

Get ready to experience the formula for answered prayers: Prayer Plus Faith, Equals Miracles!

INTRODUCTION

Why do others seem to enjoy life while it seems you are simply enduring life? Why do some people always end up on top of the world while it seems to others that the world is on top of them?

I have also searched for answers to these questions all of my days as a frequent and consistent church-goer. What seems to separate those who enjoy life and those who struggle with various aspects of day-to-day living?

The answer is not that some people are lucky or just by happenstance never have to worry. I believe that the answer is through a commitment to PRAYER and increased FAITH. Furthermore, you must have a clear perspective of God's will or plan for your life.

They say you should never answer a question with a question but you can find out where you stand by asking yourself: 1. Do I pray consistently? 2. How big is my faith? 3. What is God's will and purpose in my life? Have I been praying my own will and not God's will?

Those who incorporate prayer and have faith to believe can open up the portal to seeing a change in their daily lives. I haven't always been consistent in my own prayer life and it took me a good while to understand God's plan for my life. When I made the commitment to prayer and became obedient to God's Word then things started to change for the better. With some effort and time commitment, I know that the same can happen for you.

If you are reading this book, it's safe to say congratulations on your first step to 31 days of fervent prayer which is a faith journey.

In spite of the turmoil we go through or the things we lack, prayer is our secret weapon in a chaotic world! In some schools and in our government, prayer is not allowed. When we don't pray as a unified body, then violence, crime, natural disaster and political unrest continues.

When times get tough the solution is simple...Pray your way out by actively pursuing faith. Prayer opens doors. If you desire to see the promises of God come to pass, you must have a positive expectation that after you pray something will happen. This expectation comes through faith and knowing God's plan and will for your life. It is easy to become faithless in a society where faith is often preached but seldom practiced.

Some people can pray all the prayers in the world only to find that they are praying amidst, or rather they lack the required faith to believe. We don't pray FOR faith but we must pray with faith! How does faith grow? It grows through our day-to-day experiences with God. The challenges that you go through in life should increase not decrease your faith.

Hebrews 11:6 declares that *without faith, it is impossible to please God.* When you lack faith, it is quite difficult to be who God called you to be. Also, you limit God's ability to do something miraculous in your life. Lacking faith can consist of anything from self-defeating thoughts to crippling emotions such as fear or anger. Life is an uphill battle and you must fight each and every day to stay encouraged. You cannot get angry or harbor resentment because everything isn't working out the way you think it should. You must become equipped through prayer to accept God's will and plan for whatever comes your way. You cannot afford to lose the battle of life to discouragement fear, anger, and doubt!

Hebrews 11:6 further reveals to us that God is a *rewarder of those that diligently seek Him.* There is a certain level of expectancy we can rest in and obtain God's rewards through our commitment to prayer and reading the Word of God.

The reality is that in life you will get discouraged from time to time but it's important not to dwell there. You've got to believe that through determination, you can and you will walk in total victory! In times of trouble, you can't rely on anyone else's faith but instead practice growing your own faith. This is the moment you can then command every negative thought to become subject to the power and authority of the Holy Ghost!

There are many things that prayer and faith can do together. When there is a "marriage" between the two: It fills us with the Holy Ghost; fosters repentance; it sanctifies; saves from sin; heals the sick; saves the lost; brings forth blessings; produces good works and most importantly, redirects the fiery darts of the enemy.

How do we release our faith at this level? Ephesians 6:16 *says "take up the shield of faith, with which you can extinguish all the flaming arrows of the evil one."* We release faith through prayer and God inspired actions. You do this by holding up the shield of faith as God's Word commands. This is a good time to make a declaration by repeating: "I just don't want to simply believe in God; I want to believe that

He can and He will--without a hint of doubt--move in my life."

So why write this book? This all sounds simple enough, right? My husband and I have been pastoring a church for quite some time. What we have experienced is when we teach about faith, many simply talk about the faith they possess and often read about faith in God's Word. The tough part to face is that when trials do come, some of the toughest believers are the first to run.

This is always the easier solution instead of using our God-given abilities to *properly* confront the enemy. I use the word "properly" very narrowly because there is an "improper" way to deal with matters of the heart and life challenges in general. I'm not talking about running in the literal sense. One of the ways we run is by making excuses not to do as God commands in his Word. This often leads to placing blame on others for our mishaps and misfortunes.

It is important to find the real root cause of life's issues. Many people are stuck and do not know God's will or plan for their life. When it comes to ministry, some even find themselves wandering in the wilderness only to look in the mirror and see that they have had 12 pastors and visited 20 churches in a lifetime, to find there's still no progression only oppression.

It is one thing to simply go to church week after week, but it's something entirely different to depend on faith and wholeheartedly believe that Jesus Christ is Lord. The key is to know that being a believer or church-goer alone is not where faith ends! Romans 1:17 teaches us that *"the just man shall live by faith."* To be victorious against the fiery darts that the enemy throws your way means to live by serious faith.

What difficult problems are you facing? What you can expect to find in this book are 31 prayers and journal space to help focus your prayers and break free from oppression, depression and demonic forces. In my time in ministry, I have met many people who lost faith and believe that prayer doesn't work because very little works out in their favor. If you have become discouraged, just know that prayer is never a waste time. God hears you and He sees your tears.

As I reflect back to my younger days in high school math classes, to solve a problem we had to match the right numbers with the correct variables. Each time I got the right answer my confidence grew. I then became eager for the next set of problems to solve. Sometimes, I would get the problem correct and other times I would get it wrong. When I would get an incorrect answer, my confidence could not help but turn into discouragement. It is the same way when you lose faith. It is then easy to lose your desire to pray.

When you face difficult life problems you can pick up this book. After praying, you will walk away feeling victorious and become better equipped to face many of life's most difficult challenges. There is space to write out your thoughts at the end of each prayer, where you can record and keep track of what happened to your situation after you pray.

Freedom from oppression begins with one simple solution and that is prayer. I believe that when we fail to pray we become powerless; we only become powerful through faith and prayer. You can be free from the strongholds of financial pressures, worry, bitterness, and sin—or whatever situation you might be facing. It's time to go from oppression to progression. Jesus performed many miracles in the New Testament. Similar miracles can happen for you.

The prayers here can also serve as your guide to finding a pathway to daily devotion with God. When I get hungry, I don't go to any restaurant to eat but I eat what I crave and eat until I get full. Keep at the forefront of everyday living that prayers feed the spirit. Pray until you are full and get what you need!

My prayer for you is that you learn how not to repeat a prayer but fervently pray until you are well fed. There is no particular order; you can mix up the days or read the prayers in order day by day.

You can pray these prayers silently or out loud; alone or in a group. As you pray, get in a posture that connects your actions with these power-filled and passionate prayers. You may want to kneel or lay out prone. Effective prayer doesn't have to be complicated with fancy words but you can pray with the most simplistic and sincere words. Whatever you decide, your ultimate goal is to focus your prayers. Give God your heart and strive to be obedient to the call of prayer.

You might not be led just pray for yourself but to pray these prayers for someone else. Either way, these prayers can help turn around your negative situation. Better days are ahead—believe it and receive it! As you pray, I touch and agree with you but I want you to speak and believe it too. Accept that everything that happens or doesn't happen in your favor may or may not be God's will and plan for you.

Some will pray and it will seem like everything they pray for yields a positive result. Others will pray and it will seem as if nothing will happen. The question posed to you is will you trust God enough not to give up? When we decide to stay in the game of life, we must stay in faith. If you don't win, it's going to be alright. Keep praying until something breaks.

James: 4:6 says *"you have not because you ask not."* Just know that you are free to ask or pray for whatever you need and want. The flipside to this is that there are times when we will pray amidst. Rather, there's no guarantee that you will get everything you want in life. In faith, we aren't just trusting God for something tangible, but we must condition our minds to trust Him to carry us through the hard times.

Hebrews 5:7 reveals *"during the days of Jesus' life on earth, he offered up prayers and petitions with fervent cries and tears to the one who could save him from death, and he was heard because of his reverent submission."*

We must look at prayer as a privilege, not an obligation. Instead of praying for things, begin to pray God's will for your life. The journey to 31 days of fervent prayer will not be easy. Know that many attacks from the enemy will come.

Lastly, I want to encourage you that when it seems nothing is happening to just keep praying. In the days and times we live in and with all that is happening around us, prayer is more than necessary.

Get ready to make a conscious effort to change your life through heartfelt prayer.

Now Entering –

31 Days of Fervent Prayer

fer·vent

['fərvənt]

ADJECTIVE

1. having or displaying a passionate intensity:
   "a fervent disciple of tax reform"
   synonyms: impassioned · passionate · intense · vehement · ardent · sincere · fervid · heartfelt · enthusiastic · zealous · fanatical · hardcore · wholehearted · avid ·

- archaic

  hot, burning, or glowing.

DAY
1

"The LORD has done it this very day; let us rejoice today and be glad."

Psalms 118:24

Eternal God; Merciful Father; what a glorious day this is in You! I am grateful for the freedom to be able to worship You in Spirit and in truth! I lift up my hands unto You as a sacrifice of praise and render thanks and glory unto You. Help me to know You in the fullness of Joy. I thank You in advance for joy unspeakable.

I recognize that You O God, are the giver of life. I am grateful for yet another day in the land of the living! Someone didn't get the benefit of life this morning but I am honored that You saw fit to grant me the benefit of life. This is a new day that I commit to starting a new journey in You! In everything, I give thanks, for this is the will of God concerning me!

You inhabit the praises of Your people! So, God today--occupy my praise! I am grateful for the freedom to worship and praise You when I want and how I want! I repent for anything that I may have done that goes against Your Word. Cleanse me from my sins and all unrighteousness.

Every day going forward, I ask that You come into my heart and dwell there continually. It is my earnest desire that Your presence reign over my life. I will remain confident in knowing that Your grace and mercy sustains me daily.

I appreciate the life You have given me and I'm thankful for the many blessings that I will receive in the future. Help me O God to shift my focus. From this day onward, I will make space for You in my own personal worship time.

Where there is confusion, I pray for clarity. Where there is doubt, I pray for a sense of blessed assurance.

I realize that I have not made it this far on my own account but it is Your mercy that can deliver me from the bondages of sin. When I am faced with opposition, my hope is that You would give me peace in the midst of hopelessness. I rest in knowing that You are a God that provides encouragement, even in moments of profound discouragement.

I thank You that Your son Jesus Christ died on the cross for me. Bring comfort in knowing that You cover me daily with Your precious blood. Because Christ has already paid a heavy price for my sins, I am already victorious! I now walk into my new found victory!

Your Word declares NO weapon formed against me can prosper. Protect me and those that I love from all hurt, harm, and danger! As You build a hedge of protection around me and my loved ones, thwart every trap of satan.

I praise You for profound peace-- for a sound mind, power, and love. Please O God, incline Your ear to hear this prayer.

It is in the matchless name of Jesus I do pray, Amen.

My Daily Prayer Journal

DAY 2

"Do not be anxious about anything, but in every situation, by prayer and petition, with thanksgiving, present your requests to God."

Philippians 4:6

Arise, dear soul! Early do I seek Your countenance. I delight in You O Lord; Today I carefully reflect on who You are! You are the Lord that has all power to prevail.

You are the only God that speaks to me in the still of the night and before whom I can stand, kneel or lay before in prayer. You make all things new! I value the many chances You have given me to start life over again.

Teach me how to remain humble and remain patient in moments of frustration. Give me a spirit of boldness to ask You for the desires of my heart. I will not hesitate out of fear to request through prayer the things that I want and need. God, I acknowledge that if it's not in Your perfect will for me to have, then I decline anything that you don't want me to have. I receive with my arms wide open whatever You have for me.

You have done many great things thus far in my life and have made them known! I will walk in Your magnificence! I am fearfully and wonderfully made in Your image and I bask in that! It is not my own personal achievements that are important but my personal commitment that I am making to live for You, Oh God.

Let all of my words and deeds demonstrate who You are in my life in a mighty way! Consume me with Your love. I ask that You then fill me with Your love as You place that same love inside of me to spread to others around me.

I thank You for Your divine protection from my enemies. I know that it is by Your grace and mercy that I am kept out of harm's way. If You hadn't been my shield and my help, calamities would have engulfed me and I would not be healthy and safe.

Give me the grace to study Your Word and apply it faithfully to my life journey. I call to You from the depths of my heart and my supplication will ascend to You. Continue to safeguard me and those around me from the wiles of satan and powers of darkness. Keep me from sin, disgrace, and wickedness. Without You, I can do nothing! Help me to discover my purpose and unveil Your plan for my life as I begin my work in Your name. My gifts and callings are not for myself, but for Your glory and divine majesty.

O God, preserve my soul, mind, senses, and thoughts. Safeguard me against the destruction of my enemies that they cannot harm me secretly, nor openly. Oppose those who seek out to harm me with cunning violence or malice. Shield me from impurities and disorderly conduct.

I will refrain from all forms of greed and thinking shameful thoughts. I only desire to do whatever is pleasing to You and useful to me, that I may live on purpose and earnestly serve You. Look upon me with Your eyes of mercy. You are the Savior of the world! Enlighten my heart and eyes as I stand in the light of Your grace, which ascends above me.

I pray this prayer the matchless name of Christ Jesus. I declare and believe all of these things to be so! Amen!

My Daily Prayer Journal

DAY
3

*"But when you pray, go into your room, close the door
and pray to your Father, who is unseen. Then your Father,
who sees what is done in secret, will reward you."*

Matthew 6:6

Eternal God, early will I seek Thee! I look to the hills from which comes all of my help. Every day I will worship Thee. I will not cease in my praise. Your praises shall forevermore be in my mouth. May the praises of my lips I bring before You at this early hour, be acceptable in Your sight.

Blessed be Your divine power and might; For Thou hast shielded me with Your hand against the perils of this world and safeguarded me against the evil one. I magnify Your goodness and the wonders of Your glory. Lead, guide and direct me to the path of Your commandments that I may live a life that is pleasing to You.

I call upon You with all my heart to preserve me this day against all dangers of the world. May Your holy angels keep charge over me day after day. Protect me with Your shield.

I will not be overcome by the trials and tribulations that plague this world. I consecrate and dedicate myself entirely to Your holy will, inwardly and outwardly. Make me a living sacrifice, holy and acceptable unto you. Govern my heart, mind, and spirit. Give me a deeper understanding of Your Word and Your ways as I come to know and understand You O God.

I await the manifestations of Your promises! Help me to walk freely in You, no longer bound by my past, but walking confidently into my future. I declare that I have a renewed mind, clean heart and right spirit within.

Even in the midst of the enemy's plans to ruin my day, I ask that You immediately cease any plans for my detriment from prospering. I believe that all things are working together for my good.

Continue to prepare me and mold me for the journey of life. May your never-ending favor be evident in all that I do. Allow me to walk in accordance with Your word so that my light will shine ever so brightly in a dark and cruel world. I will be a light that draws others to You as I testify of Your goodness to those that are lost.

For every valley experience, help me to appreciate the bad with the good. As I grow in faith, I realize that You are preparing me for greater. I have purposed in my mind that I will become who You have called me to be.

If You are for me, then nobody in the world can come against me! So, today I go forward with great expectations to see miracles in ways that I have never experienced. Thank You in advance for moving the hand of adversity and clothing me with peace, love, and joy. Fill me up with more of You, O Lord!

It is an honor a privilege to have the freedom to pray this prayer. Seal this prayer with Your blessings. It is through Jesus Christ that I pray this prayer. Amen.

My Daily Prayer Journal

DAY
4

*"But I tell you, love your enemies and pray for those who
persecute you."*

Matthew 5:44

O Lord the God of my ancestors, You are the ruler of the kingdoms on earth. You are powerful and mighty and no one can stand against you! Forgive me for every sin which I have committed not only against You, but against my brothers and sisters in Christ.

Preserve me from the deadly pestilence that walks in the darkness and deliver me from the snares of the enemy. Protect me from the temptation and terror of satan for You are my strong fortress, my shield, my sword, and buckler.

Everlasting God, I honor you for Your divine power that has preserved me from all injury and danger. I will overtake my enemies with love and declare that I am powerful and unstoppable! I acknowledge that You are my keeper, provider, and protector. It is Your mercy alone that has protected me up until this very day.

Create in me a clean heart as I grow to love those that have wronged me. Help me to forgive those that have despitefully used me and persecuted me with the intention of harming me.

Encourage and restore the mind of those who battle with a tormented soul! Give them eyes to see You even in the midst of instability and calamity. Move by Your power and renew a right spirit within those who struggle with unstable emotions. If it's me O God, help me to fight negative feelings and prevent self-destructing behaviors from festering and becoming a hindrance to my growth in You!

Touch the wayward and rebellious mind; give clarity to those thoughts and things which You have called me to do! Remove barriers to my forgiveness towards others. Pull down every stronghold and cast aside un-forgiveness in my heart. Instill in me the love of Christ and incline my heart to love others even when I know they have wronged me. I will not retaliate with evil for evil but respond with the same love that Christ exemplified when He died on Calvary and shed his blood for my sins.

I bind up every spiritual attack that keeps me bound mentally, physically, emotionally, spiritually and financially!

Replace worry, fear, and doubt with the fruits of the Spirit. Increase my faith and cause me to trust in You, O God. All of my help comes from You O Lord, maker, and creator of the heaven and earth.

It is through Your Son Jesus Christ that I boldly ask You to honor these day to day petitions of prayers. Amen.

My Daily Prayer Journal

DAY
5

*"This is the confidence we have in approaching God:
that if we ask anything according to his will, He hears us."*

1 John 5:14

Most powerful and loving Father above, I give all thanks, glory, and honor unto You. I will go forth today with a praise in my heart that flows effortlessly from my lips. You are El Shaddai, the God Almighty! It is a privilege to worship and Praise You, Father God. All that I search for and need is found in You. Today I will press forward and tackle my day, boldly and with confidence.

Show me how to put on the full armor of God: Truth, righteousness, the Word, peace, faith, and salvation. Thank You for love, joy, inner peace and a sound mind. I declare that I am more than a conqueror through Christ Jesus that lives in me. I am grateful for every promise fulfilled through Your mighty Word. In spite of what's going around me, I will continue to stand -- Unshaken, steadfast and unmovable!

Grant me the grace to accept Your will concerning my life. I accept the things I cannot change. For every barren situation, I know the outcome is working in my favor. I am clothed in Your righteousness. When the storms of life come, I will lean on Your understanding, power, and truth.

In spite of every door that's been closed, I stand in faith knowing that if it be your will, there will be another door opened. I have so many pressing desires and needs before You. Even if I don't get what I want, I know You are still able to perfect everything concerning me.

Restore, rebuild and refine me for Your glory! Give me supernatural strength to endure all things. This battle is not for me to fight, but You will stand strong with me and fight for me in my weakest hour. Nothing is too big or too small for You!

O Lord, how manifold are Your works! The earth is full of Your riches. You have dominion over the earth and everything falls under Your subjection, including satan himself and his antics. In the days to come, I pray that You would meet every financial need of my household. I am grateful that Your Grace is sufficient and has kept me thus far. Your mercies are new each and every day. I surrender to Your plan for me as you illuminate the path you have purposed for my life.

I will promote peace, compassion, and love to those around me. Open my ears that I may not just hear Your holy Word, but live by Your Word with a believing heart. In my moments of distress, hear my cry unto You and hear the voice of my supplications.

I will forever rejoice and be glad all of my days. I pray this prayer in the name of Your son, Jesus Christ. Amen.

My Daily Prayer Journal

DAY
6

"Look to the LORD and his strength; seek his face always."

1 Chronicles 16:11

O Lord--Merciful God and Holy Father, I am grateful that Your goodness and mercy yet sustains me. You are the sole strength of my life. Without merit or worthiness on my part, You have preserved me from all harm and danger. I am grateful that You are a rewarder to those that diligently seek you. So I will make it my priority to carefully seek You.

For the sake of the bitter sufferings of Jesus Christ, forgive me wherever and whenever I have sinned against You this day. Cause Your Spirit to rise up in moments:

When I'm weak,

When I am fearful,

When I doubt,

When I make wrong choices or have wrong thoughts,

When I am facing financial challenges and

When I am sorrowful;

Grant me strength, peace, courage and a right way of thinking!

I won't look to man to solve my life's challenges but humbly come to You with every concern, problem, or malady.

Comfort me to rest without anxieties and worries. May the eyes of my faith behold the luster of Your countenance. When life seems dim, may You be a shining light that dispels the darkness surrounding me.

Renew my mind with the power of Your Word! Abide with me, for without you I would be subject to a world of darkness and far removed from Your saving grace.

I patiently await the manifestation of Your promises, not just for me, but for those connected to me. Let this be a moment of a newfound spiritual revival! I declare that I will not be dismayed by bleak circumstances, but remain encouraged by Your unfailing love.

Heal heavy hearts, troubled minds, and weary souls! Comfort me to know that thou, O Lord are forever with me. You are my rock, my fortress, my deliverer, my strength in Whom I will trust; You are the horn of my salvation and my strong tower. My eyes behold Your glory and I hold firm to Your promises. I bask in Your peace, love, and joy.

I pray these requests through the powerful and loving name of Jesus Christ, our risen Lord, and Savior. Amen.

My Daily Prayer Journal

DAY
7

"Now my eyes will be open and my ears attentive to the prayers offered in this place."

2 Chronicles 7:15

Almighty and all-gracious God, I come before You with thanksgiving in my heart. Enthroned above the cherubim, You are the God of all the kingdoms and the earth. For You alone created the heavens and the earth. May Your joy be an everlasting strength to carry me throughout this day.

Fill me with Your Holy Spirit that I may serve You in righteousness and in truth. Show me how to walk by faith and not by sight. Man will fail me every time, but my trust and hope remains in You. Give me a set of spiritual eyes that I may see You as I begin to see others through Your lens.

Cause my faith to soar to new dimensions. I come against suicidal thoughts, self-righteous thoughts, financial distress, and health issues; cancer, diabetes, blood disease, high blood pressure; it has no rightful place in my life!

Help me to be a good steward over my finances. I will discipline myself to spend my increase for the things that I need, not the things that I want. I will give of my substance, my 10% back to You from that which You have blessed me with.

Uncommon favor will rest on my life and those connected to me. This is my set time of favor. I release the spirit of wealth and declare divine and supernatural riches! I command every financial blessing that is assigned to me, to no longer be held back and it is released to me now!

I am grateful that You are my Keeper, my Provider, and my Protector. Whatever might be troubling me, regulate my thoughts.

Save me from the snares of the enemy so that the earth may know that You, O Lord, are the God who prevails.

Control my emotions; cause them not to be a hindrance to my growth! You've blessed me with the feeling of emotions; now help me to control them!

Guard my heart that I sin not against Thee nor defile my conscience with carnal lusts that mitigate the soul. Keep my tongue from evil and my lips from speaking foolish words that are unbecoming of believers.

I will not offend others with my words or deeds, nor backbite, judge, condemn, defame or vilify. Give me the grace to see my shortcomings and correct them. Cause me to not fall into Your judgment and condemnation.

Grant my prayer O Eternal God, for the sake of Your dear Son Jesus Christ I pray. Amen.

My Daily Prayer Journal

DAY
8

"Now to him who is able to do immeasurably more than all we ask or imagine, according to his power that is at work within us,"

Ephesians 3:20

Most Holy Trinity; God in three persons--Thou art my life, salvation and eternal joy.

If I have sinned against Thee and Thy holy commandments, I pray divine goodness would effectually cover my shortcomings and wrongdoings. Though my sins have become a crimson stain, purge me with hyssop, wash me and make me anew, that I may be whiter than snow!

I believe that Christ has arisen according to the power of the Almighty God! Today, cause this same power to rest in me! I proclaim that I am powerful! Victory is here and defeat is no longer crippling me.

I welcome the overflow of favor that's coming into my life. I realize that I am far more powerful when I walk according to the plans and purposes God has for me. Breakthroughs and blessings continue to be my birthright. From this day forward, I will live beyond the ordinary and walk in the land of favor! I understand that I am not a byproduct of my circumstances. Where I am right now does not define who I am.

Ignite the gifts lying dormant within! Stir up my purpose. Give me a willing heart and help me to tap into a supernatural faith to believe in the power of prayer. Renew my mind daily through Your Word.

Open the door to new levels of understanding of who You are O God.

There is power in trusting You and doing good to others. Help me to trust You more on this journey called life. When others mistreat me, show me how to do good in spite of how others treat me.

Teach me how to place all hope in You. I will lean not on my own understanding but put all of my trust You. Discouragement and fear are great obstacles to completing God's works. When discouragement eats away at my motivation and fear sets in to paralyze me, help me to overcome these barriers.

I know that Your Word will not come back void concerning me. Your Word is a light unto my pathway and as such, I will Your Word in my heart.

May the sublime truth of God cover me; the profound knowledge of Christ strengthen me; the unfathomable goodness of the Lord keep me. May the never-ending grace of the Father govern me; the wisdom of the Son refresh me; the power of the Holy Spirit enlighten me.

I pray that You would lift up Your countenance upon me and give me peace and hope. I do not doubt that Thou art with me, O blessed Trinity.

My Daily Prayer Journal

DAY
9

"For I know the plans I have for you, declares the LORD,
plans to prosper you and not to harm you, plans to give
you hope and a future."

Jeremiah 29:11

O how I magnify Your holy name. You are the Lord of hosts! I glorify and thank You for where I have been and where I am going. I am grateful that Your mercies are new every morning, O Lord; for You are an omnipresent God. For it is You that has so graciously kept me during this journey of life and have brought me out of the darkness into the light of day. I stand in awe of You. Your wonderful works remind me daily of Your promises that will come to pass in my life.

Thank You for being a covenant keeping God that delivers me from every dark place. I realize that it is Your Word that gives me life. I come against the weary and wounded soul. I create distance from the things that so easily beset me and refuse to be enslaved to heartache, fear, pain, and strife.

Those desires and requests that I have need of may be delayed, but because of Your Son Jesus Christ, I know they are not denied.

I ask that You begin to stretch and increase my faith. Wake up my purpose as I hold on to Your unchanging hand. Take me from my comfort zone. Because of my strengthened and renewed faith, I have high expectations for greater things to happen in my life.

You have guarded and watched over my soul as a true shepherd watches over his flock. You O God are my refuge, my strong tower, and my present help. It is in You that I put my trust. Be my salvation and my guide in the time of trouble. Defend me against evildoers and workers of iniquity. Shield me from the hands of my adversaries so that they may not touch me.

Strongholds over my life are cast down! Every attack against my mind, body, heart, soul, finances, marriage, families and relationships are defeated in the matchless name of Jesus! I command peace to overtake me and those around me.

Today, I walk with my head up, shoulders back and walk with a continuous praise on my lips because I am victorious. I look forward to a bright and prosperous future. I realize that I have been bought with a price. Your ways are not always my ways; Your plans are not always my plans.

I will build my hopes on things eternal, not on the promises of this world. I walk by faith and not by sight, with a renewed mind, rejuvenated soul and a heart full of joy!

My time and season are not in the hands of man but in Your hands O God! This is my season of prosperity. I call forth divine wealth and divine favor and command it to rest upon me and those connected to me.

I declare that I am first and not last; I am above and not beneath; I am a lender and not a borrower. Defeat, shame, guilt, and fear will no longer be my birthright! My past is over and I will not allow it to become my present or my future. Show me daily how to keep your commandments and how to sin not against Thee.

Grant me these things for the sake of Your mercy, which endures forever and ever. Amen.

My Daily Prayer Journal

*"I praise you because I am fearfully and wonderfully made;
your works are wonderful, I know that full well."*

Psalm 139:14

I am thankful for yet another day to rest in Your splendor! Your mercy O Lord rests in the heavens; Your faithfulness reaches unto the clouds. Your right hand gladdens my heart and under the shadow of Your wings, I take refuge. I lay before You emptied out.

You are omniscient and omnipresent! Your love is unconditional and never-ending. I praise You in the midst of Your magnificence that surrounds me! You have dominion over every living and breathing thing. You are gracious and merciful and all of Your creation is deemed glorious.

Today, I won't ask for anything temporal but count it all joy to marvel at Your wondrous works. I am made anew and God breathed life will overtake me. It is in Your image and likeness that I am fearfully and wonderfully made.

I will not react emotionally to negative situations but react spiritually. I will refrain from speaking negative or discouraging words, and speak only positive and encouraging words. My heart boasts in You and because of this, I am helped. Everything I touch, say and do is blessed.

Your knowledge, wisdom, and understanding are invaluable! When things don't go my way or the outcome of my situation doesn't seem to be working in my favor, I will not complain but will realize that this as the will of God concerning me.

I declare that You have better days ahead in store for me! Your Word is a consistent reminder that my present circumstances won't overtake me but cause me to rise above every negative condition.

Continue to abide in me as I abide in You. May Your face continually shine upon me and may Your grace refill, restore and replenish me.

It is in the matchless name of El Elyon--the most-high God, that I pray these prayers, Amen.

My Daily Prayer Journal

DAY
11

*"The righteous cry out, and the LORD hears them; he
delivers them from all their troubles."*

Psalm 34:17

Blessed are You O God, my Maker, my Helper, my Sustainer, my Savior, my Comforter! You O God are my Alpha and Omega; my beginning and end! There is no other God beside You or above You. O How I exalt Your name with gladness. Life is not promised. It is with exceeding joy that I am grateful to live and see yet another beautiful day.

I understand that in this earthly life that I live, there will be pressure, pain, and trouble. When I am under significant pressure, feeling pained or faced with traumatic experiences, give me the strength to stand still and turn to You O God. Help me to use wisdom and knowledge as I cope with life's issues and resist reacting with wrong actions, wrong thoughts and vile reactions that are not biblical or Godly.

Position and align me with your seamless purpose for my life. In moments where I have fallen from Your grace, restore me to my rightful place in You.

Where applicable, I declare freedom from every addiction (drugs, alcohol, gambling, tobacco, lust, perversion, a lying tongue, bad habits, disease, fear, doubt, and worry). Purify my mind; make my thoughts anew! I will not carry the weight on my shoulders resulting from demons that cause me undue stress and affliction.

Protect me from all unrighteousness. May peace, love and joy resonate deep down within me as only a touch at the very core from Your redeeming hands blocks the plan of the enemy.

Incline my heart to forever keep Your commandments. I will meditate on Your Word daily. Lead me on the path of righteousness so that I would not walk in the counsel of the ungodly, nor stand in the way of sinners. Cause me not to sit in the seat of the scornful. Create in me a heart that beats as one with You for it is only with the mind and heart of Christ that I will think and become a new creature.

I stand firm in Your unmerited favor as I justly carry out my kingdom work You have graciously ordained for me to complete. I can no longer operate as I have in the past.

Grant me Your unfailing mercy and hear my cries to You. For it is when I cry with my voice, that You hear me and lend Your ear to my supplication.

With a clear mind and heart, I place these cries of petition at Your feet. When I pray, attend to my voice, O God! I believe and decree that all things are turning around for my good.

I pray this prayer in the precious name of Yeshua HaMashiach, our Lord, and Savior Christ Jesus that I pray this daily prayer. Amen.

My Daily Prayer Journal

DAY
12

"Trust in the LORD with all your heart, and lean not to your own understanding. In all your ways submit to him, and he will make your paths straight."

Proverbs 3:5-6

Blessed be the Lord my God, who does wondrous things!

The whole earth is filled with Your glory. Today I will abound in peace, love, and joy, which only comes from You! I recognize that You O Lord, are my refuge and strength; a very present help in times of trouble. Be my shield and preserve me from all evil. It is in You that I will put my trust!

My heart rejoices and my soul shall glorify You in all Your goodness and mercy. This very day, cause me to abide in a secret dwelling place as You pour into me everything that my spirit longs for.

May Your perfect will manifest in extraordinary ways in my life. There are good and bad things happening in my personal life and in the world that surrounds me that I cannot understand. Give me the insight to hear your voice concerning every situation that I cannot comprehend. Grant me the grace to know that my thoughts are not your thoughts and Your ways are not my ways.

Where my thinking is limited, expand my mindset. Cause me not to go astray by way of wrong thinking. Keep me from following people and things that "appear" to be right but help me to follow Your perfect pathway.

I will continue to seek Your kingdom and righteousness so that all things might be added unto me! I will depend on Your immeasurable strength, stamina, perseverance, courage, and confidence as I take on the mindset of Jesus Christ.

I won't begin my day asking for material things or bringing forth petitions filled with personal issues, but I pray for a sweet rest and peace in You!

Cultivate the divine gifts and talents within me that they might be used for the edification and building of Your kingdom.

When others have failed me and let me down, show me how to rebuild my hope in things eternal. From this day forward, I vow to first love You with my whole heart. Your Word will forever be a light unto my path. Guide my steps on the paths of righteousness. I will live according to the unchanging and unfailing Word of God.

Awaken me again O Lord with a new level of rejoicing! May Your goodness and mercy continue to follow me for the rest of my days.

It is through Jesus Christ, our Lord, and Savior that I pray these prayers. Amen.

My Daily Prayer Journal

DAY
13

"And God is able to bless you abundantly, so that in all things at all times, having all that you need, you will abound in every good work."

2 Corinthians 9:8

Lord God my Savior, early will I seek Thee! It is good to give thanks unto the Lord and sing praises that are due Your name. I proclaim Your salvation on the earth and I will tell others of your marvelous works.

It is You that has blessed me and Your unfailing love that has empowered me. You are my refuge and my help. It is not by my own might but by Your might, power, and strength that I am blessed beyond measure. Your immeasurable grace has kept me. For that, I'm extremely grateful!

I will guard myself against the things which You hate and which are an abomination. I refrain from producing a proud look, a lying tongue, hands that shed innocent blood, a heart that deviseth wicked imaginations, feet that are swift in running to mischief, a false witness that speaketh lies and sowing discord amongst my brethren.

Remove my ego and all acts of selfishness. Daily shall I live in a state of repentance and humility.

I am successful in every work that runs through my hands. I leave it up to You O God to perfect everything concerning me. One thing for certain is that I will be responsible over all that You have blessed me with.

I am not be moved or shaken by the cares and woes of life. Your Word is very much alive and powerful! Give me the discipline to not simply pray to you but to sit diligently and read Your Word! Help me to understand Your Word to better apply it to every aspect of my life.

I pray against the assignment of the enemy over my life, my family, and my ministry. Satan's plans have no place or dominion over my life! For every demonic attack, vengeance will be Yours O God! I bind the spirit of heaviness, oppression, and depression.

I cast down distress and place it at Your feet. Give me stability where there is instability. I speak against anything that is contrary to Your Word that will hinder the fulfillment of Your original purpose for me. I walk in the timing and the favor of You O God. I, therefore speak deliverance in every area and I open my heart to Your divine deliverance.

I will wear a garment of praise! In the midst of turmoil, I put on garments of war, as vengeance will be yours, says the Lord of hosts! Gird me with your supernatural power and equip me with the shield of salvation. Cause Your right hand to establish me and lift up a standard through Your Word, power and might against the battle plan of every naysayer.

Today, search my heart and remove anything that does not compliment Your purpose for me. Circumstances might get uncomfortable, painful or even intimidating. But, You know exactly what I need and the moment that I have need of it!

It is during my weary seasons of life that I will cling to You. Build my character and perseverance for I know that You will shine greatly within me, and because of that, others around me will begin to see Your light reflected in me.

Hear my prayers O Lord. I place these petitions at Your feet in the name of Your son Jesus Christ, Amen.

My Daily Prayer Journal

DAY
14

*"Blessed is the one who perseveres under trial because,
having stood the test, that person will receive the crown of
life that the Lord has promised to those who love him."*

James 1:12

Praise be unto You O great and unchangeable God! Praise be unto You for Your never-ending eternal wisdom!

I thank You for another blessed day on earth; a day that I have yet to see in its entirety. I know this will be a day that I will be blessed beyond measure. I realize that there is no greater love than the love You have confessed towards me.

Your peace transcends beyond what I can see with the natural eye, even in the midst of troubled and perilous times. With an abounding joy deep within, I prevail in all things with a smile and a laughter that will flow, even in the roughest times!

I know that without faith, it is impossible to please God. I submit myself to Your more than capable hands. I now shift my focus and allow patience and virtue to take precedence over fear and worry. I remain steadfast and will not be shaken or distracted by my day-to-day circumstances.

When I look at the negativity around me, I won't be devastated or depressed by what I see. I will go beyond the veil and begin to see beyond the natural eye. When I am troubled and when my spirit is overwhelmed, I will call on You O God as my Savior.

Thank You in advance, O God, for the exchange of a crown of beauty for every coil of ashes that has been wrapped around my life. Today and every day going forward, I will wear the helmet of salvation.

I declare liberation from soul ties and generational curses over my life. By Your blood and by Your spirit, I am free from all negativity passed down from generation to generation.

Bring supernatural peace to a chaotic world. Lift heavy burdens, calm tortured minds and soothe raging souls. When I or those around me dealing with the loss of a loved one, heal the hurt and wrap the bereaved in Your loving arms!

I pray now for financial provision and declare that all of my needs are met. In this place and at this very hour, I seek only You, O Lord, in my time of need. You are the portion of mine inheritance. You are a God of more than enough and there is no task to great for you. Prosperity shall be my portion! I stand still and await Your direction in my words and deeds. It is in these times of stillness, that I can best understand Your sovereignty and hear Your subtle voice so clearly.

I wait in expectation as I welcome a mighty and bold transformation that only Your presence can bring. I embrace Your plan and begin to walk boldly into the transformed person You have destined for me to become.

Pardon my transgressions, even those which I have intentionally committed against You! With boldness and with grace, I humbly come before You in prayer and my heart is ready to receive ALL of that You have for me.

I pray these prayers in Jesus' name. Amen

My Daily Prayer Journal

DAY
15

"Watch and pray so that you will not fall into temptation. The spirit is willing, but the flesh is weak."

Matthew 26:41

Old things have passed away and behold all things have become new! O God, I thank You for waking me up today with the breath of life. Somebody didn't wake up today. I'm grateful to be on Your wake up list! I praise You for the latter days that have come and gone and the days that are ahead! I praise You in advance because I rest assured that today's victories will outweigh my defeats.

I realize that the world itself can overwhelm me with its noise and cast intrusions of evil on my mind through my thoughts. I break free from the distractions of the world that makes Your voice so hard to hear. You still reign amidst all of the clatter that exists around me.

When things in my world view me seem confusing and nothing makes sense, O Lord clarify my understanding and bring order in times of uncertainty and chaos. I refuse to be distracted from Your plan and path. In times when my flesh gets weak, impose the fruits of Your Holy Spirit. I won't give in to temptation and my shortcomings will not overtake me. You are an all knowing and all seeing God. Only You know the real and true desires of my heart.

Today, I purpose in my mind to spend quiet time with You. I realize that when I am quiet and still, these are the moments where I can openly share what has been lying dormant in my heart. I realize that there are areas of my life that need improvement. Particularly, areas where I need to bring my flesh under subjection, alignment, and agreement with the Spirit of God. Today, I put on the crown of salvation!

You have not given me a spirit of fear, which is of the enemy. You have given me a spirit of love, power, and a sound mind. Therefore, I will not be ashamed of my past sins. I repent for not following Your wise counsel and for living my life according to my own instructions.

Impart in me a perfect love that casts out fear. Strengthen my flesh and increase my spiritual growth and stamina that I might continue to live out Your plan for my life. I pray fervently for the perseverance and tenacity needed to combat the wiles of the devil.

I will not walk in the counsel of the ungodly but look to You O God for clarity in all things. If I have wronged or hurt anyone with my words, deeds or acts; free me from the spirit of offense and un-forgiveness in the hearts of others. I walk confidently in knowing that all of my concerns and wrongdoings of my flesh have been given over to You.

I am grateful for the simple things in life: Employment, food, shelter, clothes, and health. There are those around me that do lack but bless them O

God and turn their situations around in their favor, like only You can. I declare that I am blessed and my household is blessed, and will not suffer any lack.

It is in Jesus' name that I ask these petitions and prayers, Amen!

My Daily Prayer Journal

DAY
16

*"Repent, then, and turn to God, so that your sins may be
wiped out, that times of refreshing
may come from the Lord,"*

Acts 3:19

I stand in awe of You, O God! You are a God that is slow to anger, yet plenteous in mercy. Today, I ask that You would cause me not to lay down the same way I awoke this morning. Do a new work in me. Create in me a clean heart, O God; and renew a right spirit within.

I acknowledge my transgressions; my sins are ever before me. Help me to not postpone my repentance, nor put it off until the last hour, but rather cause me to turn to You this day and repent!

Renew, refine and restore my moral character. I come against the things that have held me back and prevented me from reaching Your promises. May every curse be broken over my life in the mighty name of Jesus!

Help me to rest daily in a place of repentance so that no man can unjustly charge or accuse me. I understand that anyone not willing to live in a repentive state will perish, but those that seek after repentance will have everlasting life. Purge me with hyssop and I shall be clean. Wash me whiter than snow, and I shall be made whole.

Cause seeds of iniquity, strife, discouragement, and negativity to be stripped from my life. In spite of my past and present sins, prepare for me a fertile ground for planting of an abundant harvest. Open the portals of Heaven and pour out more than I am worthy of receiving! May others around me also be blessed with this very same manner of overflow.

Cast away negative words that have been spoken over me in the earth resulting from my past sins. I come against whispering and gossip amongst the accusers of the brethren concerning my past. I break through the strongholds of the enemy. Permanently close the mouths of the naysayers and destroyers of my character that might seek to remind me of my past or present wrong doings.

Remove the guilt and shame from my heart and cause me to be confident in the newfound person I have become in You. If I am faithful over the little things You have blessed me with, I am confident You will bless me with greater. Going forward, I will refrain from repeat offenses by making poor choices. I am committed to acting as Your agent on this earth. In spite of my shortcomings, make me useful for the work of Your Kingdom.

It is in Your son Jesus name that I do humbly pray these prayers, Amen!

My Daily Prayer Journal

DAY
17

"Brothers and sisters, I do not consider myself yet to have taken hold of it. But one thing I do: Forgetting what is behind and straining toward what is ahead,"

Philippians 3:13

To whom much is given, much is required! Today I will not haphazardly or occasionally commune with You through prayer, but earnestly and diligently seek you through prayer. I realize that the most important relationship I have is not with man, but with You O God. My day-to-day fellowship with You is one that deserves my greatest expression of worship through prayer and praise.

Help me to stand on your promises! I will walk by faith and not by sight! Push me closer to what You have destined and purposed for me. As I advance into new levels and new territories, assign Your angels to protect and watch over me and those connected to me.

I won't remember the former things but look to the hills where my help comes from. I rededicate myself to You; my life will be like an altar unto You. I freely give my mind, spirit, and body to You. I will think on things that are good, right, pure and holy. Take captive of un-godly thoughts that come to rob me of my joy and remind me of my past shortcomings. I will only reflect on Your faithfulness, especially in times when my faith waivers and I am tempted to doubt.

I dedicate my eyes, ears, mouth, and heart unto You. I now see others the way You see them. Settle my ears to clearly hear Your voice above all else.

Cause the words I speak to be meaningful and life-giving. My heart will become pure and undivided. When I lose track of my emotions, I will become subject to Your Holy Spirit.

Cover my sins. Impute not my iniquities for You are a merciful God that can cleanse me from secret fault. Blot out my transgressions. Wash me thoroughly from my iniquities and restore me from my sins. I won't focus on the sins of my youth, nor my present-day transgressions.

Defeat has no place in my life. When things don't go my way, I will not get discouraged easily and give up. I declare that I am more than a conqueror through Christ Jesus! Trials and troubles may come and go, but Your love is unfailing and yet remains.

Failure will no longer be my inheritance! I arrest every demonic spirit by the power and might of Your Word! Every curse over my life is reversed! I now rest in the favor You have set in order for my life. I am liberated to move forward, boldly in the face of every obstacle and challenge.

It is by Your right hand that blessings are bestowed upon me. Through sharing my testimony with others, I won't forget to give You credit so deserving for my every success.

Equip me with a golden shield to deflect every harmful arrow that satan tries to shoot my way. When the enemy sees his arrows falling down, those plans that are not in alignment with God's will for my life will be severed, never to afflict me again!

Open up the portals of heaven! Cause my prayers to not be earthbound, but to quickly ascend into supernatural heavenly realms.

May these prayers be acceptable unto You. For Christ's sake, I pray these prayers. Amen.

My Daily Prayer Journal

DAY
18

"And without faith it is impossible to please God, because anyone who comes to him must believe that he exists and that he rewards those who earnestly seek him."

Hebrews 11:6

You are the Almighty God, with whom there is no variableness and neither a shadow of turning; from whom every good and perfect gift cometh!

You are omnipotent and gracious! I believe that You are omnipresent and ever present in my own life. I hold steadfast to Your promises. You are the God that heals, lifts burdens, and breaks yokes! You are the God that answers by fire. Burn up everything in my life that is not like you! I have witnessed Your miraculous works and I choose to believe that You are God, and God alone!

You, O God are the author and finisher of my faith. My current outlook on life will change and I am confident that You are with me. I understand that it is not enough to just say that I believe. Today, I make necessary changes to my life through faith and God inspired actions that show I believe!

You are an all-seeing and all-knowing God. You, O God know my every heart's desire. You know the state of my emotional distress and the turmoil I face each day. I give all of my burdens and worries over to You. May a calmness and confidence that wasn't there before take a deep root within me.

You see the attacks of the enemy and the struggles of my flesh. I place everything at Your feet-

-not just my burdens, but works of iniquity and works of the flesh that I struggle to overcome.

Living a life of total and complete faith can be challenging. In this day and time, there are people around me who choose to live without faith. Implant and maintain in my heart a true knowledge of Your Son, Jesus Christ, and help me to increase my faith.

I view challenging circumstances through the lens of hope and faith. When I face opposition, I will not falter but remain active in my faith through exercising patience and hope.

Grace me to become steadfast and un-moveable. I declare that I will walk and talk by faith and not by sight.

Rekindle a spark of faith in my heart as You begin a greater work in me. Fill me with the full knowledge of You through wisdom and spiritual understanding. Help me to remain faithful and loyal in all that I say and do.

Give me the encouragement and direction that I need through Your Word. I commit to making Your Word the basis of my faith. My actions will revolve around fulfilling my obligations to edify the body of Christ and build the Kingdom of God. Teach me how not to waiver in my commitments, but to hear and obey Your voice.

Grant me the knowledge of salvation and allow the forgiveness of my sins. Strengthen my weakened faith! Restore it with faith the size of a mustard seed; water my seeds of faith so that it might grow and that I become rooted and grounded in You.

Protect me O God so that I am not led astray by the errors, schisms, and heresies of the world. Preserve me from superstitions and false doctrines that I may neither err, nor doubt in any area of faith. Prevent my faith from becoming lifeless, inactive, or without fruit. Cause my faith to remain active, energetic, as I begin to focus on serving God's people in love.

Instill in me a desire to endure until the end of my faith journey which is my soul's salvation.

I receive Your glory today! With a clear heart and mind, I place this prayer petition before You and justly believe everything Your Word says concerning me.

In Jesus name, I earnestly pray this prayer, Amen!

My Daily Prayer Journal

DAY
19

"Let us examine our ways and test them, and let us return to the LORD."

Lamentations 3:40

You are the King of King and Lord of Lords. Nothing will stand in the pathway of giving Your name glory, honor and praise. Today, I will openly and honestly examine myself, my thoughts and my ways.

Your Word declares whom the Son sets free, is free indeed! I am free because I invite Your Spirit to dwell within. Cleanse me from all unrighteousness and deliver me from the bondages of sin. Impose the fruits of the spirit over my life. Instead of sowing seeds of discord, malice, envy, and strife; help me to spread seeds of hope, faith, prosperity, joy and love.

When I fall short in my ministry, personal commitments and fail to obey Your commandments, You yet remain a covenant keeping God. Change my inner heart and deliver me from bitterness, shame, pride, satanic strongholds, addictions, ungodly soul ties, toxic relationships and limiting circumstances. Today and going forward, I choose to walk in my purpose. I will not be anxious nor settle for less than I deserve. My ministry, relationships and ideas will thrive!

Show me the individuals who do not have my best interest at heart. Release me from the spirit of manipulation and control of people. Cause me to realize that I don't have to follow the crowd, especially when the crowd is headed in the wrong direction; but will condition my mind to remain separate and apart from people that are not Godly.

I repent for the moments where I have bowed down in worship to idols, participated in religious hypocrisies and placed faith in things of this world. Forgive me for the times I fell vulnerable to displaying a wrong attitude and wrong spirit.

Return me to a place of right living and genuine worship. You are a forgiving God that can turn things around for my good and for Your glory!

Baptize me with Your Holy Spirit for I am sin-stained, but You are the Lord that can wash away my sins--the God whom the heavens cannot encompass. I release my cares, concerns, issues, problems, and worries over to You O God.

When I struggle with deciding to do wrong over right and find myself drifting far away from You, cause my spirit-man fall into alignment with Your Holy Spirit. When I have wrong thoughts, I will begin to meditate on Your Word.

This day and every day going forward, I open my heart and mind to receive from You. It is in Jesus' name that I humbly pray these prayers. Amen!

My Daily Prayer Journal

DAY
20

"But seek first his kingdom and his righteousness, and all these things will be given to you as well."

Matthew 6:33

O Gracious and Blessed God, who has commanded me above all things to first seek Your kingdom and righteousness, grant me Your unfailing grace as I begin my day with worship. I submit to You through my acts of obedience by faith and choose to live a holy life according to Your Word. As I start this day, I will begin by seeking the fullness of Your grace by the power of Your omnipotent name! There is no other name above You.

I will not ask today for secular things of this world, but earnestly pray and seek after things eternal. I pray now, that not my own 'will', but that Your 'will' would be exemplified throughout my life.

Your Word declares that You would give me the desires of my heart. I have many personal desires and needs of the flesh, yet today I refrain from seeking Your face through prayer out of selfishness in pursuit of my own agenda. Instead, I will seek Your face daily, through prayer for being the God that heals, delivers and sets free! As I choose to worship and consecrate my life through prayer, I know You are more than able to supply my needs.

Help me to become and remain meek in spirit and humble at heart. As I yearn after Your righteousness, it is through humility that I will learn how to worship You in a new and unusual way.

In moments when I suffer persecution and tribulation, help me to overcome those things and individuals that rise up against me by Your power and might,. Nothing will cause me to waiver in my faith or prompt me to act out of my character or change my daily walk with You.

Deliver me O God from all powers of darkness that plague my life through Your Son Jesus Christ, in whom I am redeemed by His blood. Protect me from all offenses of man that have scandalized my name. Even in the midst of this, help me to walk upright and live a holy life that is pleasing unto You.

Give me the strength to endure such revelings and undeserved malignings, such as slander and scandal with patience and longsuffering. I loose the shackles of mental anguish and physical pain that afflicts me and those around me, in a sinful world.

I make the declaration that it doesn't matter what man says about me, but You are the center of my life! I open my heart to receive from You O God and give You Your rightful place to be the Lord over my life. I release to You my job, my family, my ministry and my time so that I can use my giftings and talents to build the kingdom.

I reflect on 1 Chronicles 4:10 and pray the very same prayer that Jabez prayed: Bless me, expand my territory, protect me from dangers seen and unseen, and may the God that I serve and believe in, be with me in words, deeds, and actions.

Help me to be righteous and display love towards others and avoid taking on evil motives, desires and actions. Guard my thoughts! Fill my mind and heart with the same love and forgiveness You have extended towards me so that I might genuinely forgive others. I will keep a positive attitude and think only good thoughts about my negative circumstances.

I will not put anything or anyone before You, O God. The Word of God prevails over my life! I will forever exalt Your name! It is in Jesus' name that I pray this prayer, Amen.

My Daily Prayer Journal

DAY
21

"No one can serve two masters. Either you will hate the one and love the other, or you will be devoted to the one and despise the other. You cannot serve both God and money."

Matthew 6:24

God be merciful to me -- a sinner saved by grace! If I have put all of my hopes in things of this world, forgive me for not walking on Your path of righteousness.

You are the true and living God. Exodus 20:3 commands that I should place no other God before You. Keep me from worshipping idol gods. I will refrain this very day from thinking negative thoughts and ideas. I pray today for a clean heart and a right spirit within.

I will not bow my knees to anything that is not like God. Grant me a peace that surpasses all understanding. I realize that You are a jealous God and I cannot serve the living God and idols at the same time. I will stand firm on Leviticus 26:1 which affirms that I should not give credence to idols and graven images, nor should I bow down to it.

The Word of God declares that the love of money is the root of all evil. Help me to not fall prey to worshiping money but to serve You O God and God alone. I will not put my hopes in what money can buy, but put all of my hopes and desires in the things of God.

I will purpose in my heart today to give far more than I receive. I believe that as I give to my ministry and to the poor, that You O God will restore all that has been lost down through the years.

You are only wise God that supplies all of my needs! I speak miracles in my health and finances. I believe this also for my family and friends. There is so much going on around me in the world today beyond my control. I pray for an abundance of peace in communities and in the world.

I thank and praise You O God for open doors; I thank and praise You for the doors that have been shut and sealed for my divine protection! Help me to leave the past behind. I will not re-open any door that Your hands have closed.

I thank You for moving mountains and I believe that no matter what stands in my way, I am victorious. Because of my obedience and spiritual discipline, I will see breakthroughs manifest in my life as Your Word declares it to be so! I will walk in Your promises and bask in Your many blessings!

I am thankful for grace and will forever appreciate Your thoughts, heart and kindness towards me!

I pray that Your grace will continue to abound with me, in me and through me! I pray for a peace that that surpasses my own understanding.

117

I wholeheartedly believe every prayer and petition shall come to pass. It is in Jesus' name I ask these things and wholeheartedly pray these prayers, Amen!

My Daily Prayer Journal

"Persecuted, but not abandoned, struck down, but not destroyed."

2 Corinthians 4:9

All things are under Your divine control. There is no problem that is too difficult for You to handle. There is no circumstance above You and beyond Your control. No other God reigns above You! I believe in Your Word and throughout my life I have experienced manifestations of Your Word. I am certain that even in perilous times, You would never leave me or forsake me.

Help me to understand that the trials and tribulations I have gone through were necessary to mold my character and cultivate the gifts within me.

People have lied to me and they have even lied on me; others have talked about me, mistreated me, defiled my character and sought to kill my reputation. Others have purposely and repeatedly stabbed me in the back in hopes that it would lead to my demise. Today is the day that every assignment has been canceled!

Many have tried to oppress, torment, intimidate and abuse my kindness. Today, every trap, plan, and plot has been terminated through the blood of Jesus Christ! The enemies' assignment has been voided and canceled.

I pray now that every negative and untruthful word spoken over my life is reversed! I realize that the opinions of others do not define who I am in Christ.

There were moments when I fell to sin because of the damaging words that others spoke over me. I thank You, O God that I will no longer be sidetracked by moments of sorrow and deep despair caused by painful words and actions of others. For it is in these very moments that my faith grows stronger in You. Every time my character was assassinated and cast down in the spirit, You safeguarded me from the snares of the enemy.

It is rarely easy but I freely forgive and release my spirit from the bitterness that has accumulated in my heart for many years. I understand that I must genuinely forgive, in order to be forgiven.

I am appreciative of the new mercies You have shown me today, and will show me every day going forward. I will purpose my heart to bask in the unconditional love that You have for me, not the negative plans that others have for me.

I will remain full of joy and peace that goes beyond my understanding. It is in the precious and powerful name of Jesus Christ that I pray these prayers and declare these words to be so, Amen!

My Daily Prayer Journal

DAY
23

*"For it is God who works in you to will and to act in order
to fulfill his good purpose."*

Philippians 2:13

Eternal God, You are the One who created the Heavens and earth; Who in all of Your infinite wisdom formed man in Your image and likeness, and breathed the breath of life into all living things! Nobody has been deemed worthy enough to die for my sins. You died for our sins so that we could all have everlasting life. You are the Almighty God who sits high, and You look down low! O God, open the portals of heaven, shower me with grace anew, and endow me with brand new mercies!

Thank You for being an Almighty God that forgives, delivers and sets free! The power of the enemy has been broken over my life, over my mind, and over my relationships.

I understand that doing Your will begins with my own spiritual discipline and desires. O God, mold and shape my attitude, belief and desires. I know that inner changes are needed in order to result in faith-filled actions. Give me the desire to follow Your infinite wisdom and instruction.

I am willing to be humble and remain in a state of humility all of my days ahead. I will be open to greater opportunities in You and move at Your direction. I will not allow my material possessions or status to prevent me from doing Your will.

You are the epitome of long-suffering! Better days are ahead for me! I might have faced significant discouragement in my life, but I will never give up hope in Your promises. I wholeheartedly believe that my turning point is not too far ahead! I won't look back on people, places and things that have prevented me from seeking our Your plan for my life.

When the chaos and calamities come to overtake my mind, it is the power of Your Word that will keep my sanity. Today, I stand firm in You; I rest in You when I am weary and grow tired from the cares of life! It is in You that I find strength and courage press forward. I will depend on the gifts that You have placed inside of me to obey Your Word and to do Your will.

Because of my sacrificial offerings, I will see the salvation of the Lord!

I declare all of these things to be so, in the mighty and matchless name of Christ Jesus! Amen!

My Daily Prayer Journal

DAY
24

"So if the Son sets you free, you will be free indeed."

John 8:36

This is the day that Lord has made; I will rejoice and be glad, for this is the will of God concerning me! This is a new day where I shall walk into multiple blessings as I accomplish those things which You have purposed for my life! Usher me into a time of refreshing; a time that can only come from basking in Your glory!

Thank You for Your favor and loving kindness that rests upon me. Your Word declares that old things have passed away and behold, all things have become new.

I am an overcomer by the words of my testimony. Today, I break free from evil control, addictions, generational curses, debt, poverty, and abuse. I declare further that I am free from depression, suicide, and unclean thoughts. Satanic oppression will no longer control me. I am liberated and walk in a new found freedom in every area of my life!

Grant me the grace to be responsible over my money so that poverty and lack will not consume my household. I will educate myself and grab hold to kingdom precepts that will teach me how to be a good steward of everything You have blessed me with. I will sow back into the kingdom of God my time, talent and money. Instill within me a desire to give to the poor and less fortunate. Through my giving, my enemies will begin to bless me; and the devour that seeks to destroy me will be overtaken!

Tears of joy will replace tears of sadness! Abundance and wealth will replace poverty and debt. Peace of mind will replace worry and anxiety.

I welcome new found freedom into my life. Through Your Word, I am no longer bound. I am liberated in You!

May the LORD forever make his face shine upon me and be gracious unto me.

It is in the mighty, magnificent and matchless name of Christ Jesus do I pray these prayers! Amen.

My Daily Prayer Journal

DAY
25

"I have been crucified with Christ and I no longer live, but Christ lives in me. The life I now live in the body, I live by faith in the Son of God, who loved me and gave himself for me."

Galatians 2:20

Today is an amazing day in You, O Lord! I will rejoice and be glad! I will give thanks in all things! Wake up my faith, O God.

I realize that self-pleasing desire is the greatest obstacle between me and my salvation, as it is in the nature of man to desire to please him/herself. I know that I cannot save myself by my works, but I must become one with Christ! Today, I completely surrender every selfish desire and ambition to the perfect will of God!

I believe that the Word of God is the infallible truth! I will make it a practice to engage in real and true repentance, not just today but every day! I no longer just ask for forgiveness of sins, but openly express my desire for inner change that conforms to the will of God! Help me to understand that it is the surrendering of my own control to the power and will of the Holy Spirit. This is just the beginning of being crucified with Christ!

I understand that I must be born again in order to see the kingdom of God. Where I have failed in this area, grant me Your grace O God! Give me the grace to replace the old sinful man. Help me to understand that it is through Your gift of grace that I can be born again and be made anew!

Satan must drop his weapons and flee! My prayer is that the hurt are comforted, the lost may be found and that the discouraged would be encouraged; broken hearts are mended; the sick shall become well and the bound will be set free! Relationships will be restored, and homes are blessed as families are reconciled with another.

I pray that this covenant prayer between me and the Lord and Savior Jesus Christ, would be strengthened!

It is in the mighty name of Jesus Christ I pray, Amen.

My Daily Prayer Journal

DAY 26

"The Lord will grant that the enemies who rise up against you will be defeated before you. They will come at you from one direction, but flee from you in seven."

Deuteronomy 28:7

Today is a blessed day in You O God...I will rejoice! You are Jehovah Nissi; my banner, my shield, my vindicator, and my protector. You are the most-high God and the establisher of the earth. I know that I have been bought with a price. My prayer this day is that You would overtake me with Your love, peace, and Your joy!

I will not focus on negative circumstances or negative words that have been planted in the earth, but look at the God who controls these circumstances! Although the enemy hates my God-given purpose, I still walk in unprecedented favor. Set me on high places. No matter what has been spoken over my life, clear my paths and make my ways perfect!

Satan comes to steal, kill and destroy what I am building and the promises that I have in Christ. I realize that the enemy will oftentimes use family members and friends to attack me. I come against works of the evil one by way of people to destroy my destiny in Christ.

Thank You O God for the authority that You have given me through Your Word to trample over my those who oppose me. I come against anyone or anything that has attacked me because of jealousy, competition, envy or hate.

Make war against the kingdoms of darkness and defeat the tricks of the adversary. You have seen my tears; You have comforted me in my moments of crying and deep despair. I don't have to fight on my own accord because I know that You will fight for me, O God! You know every plot and plan of the enemy that seeks to kill, steal and destroy me and those connected to me.

I pray now that going forward no harm or evil will come near me! Those things that follow me from my past that were set out to destroy me will no longer prosper.

I declare now that the portals of heaven will be opened up for me. Assign warring angels to my ministry, my household, and my finances.

When my enemy comes upon me to eat my flesh, may You cause them to stumble and fall. The enemy desires my feet to slip and desires that the plans for my life would fail. O God, do not allow my feet to slip! Every evil word spoken over my life, purpose and destiny has been terminated and canceled.

I pray according to Your Word that where my enemies have planted seeds of discord, that You O God would cancel every assignment designed to curse my progression. Confuse the plans of the enemy. My enemies will not rise up against me.

I am the head and not the tail. I will not be discouraged, but I am encouraged. I will not dwell on who man says I am, but I stand firm on Your Word and I am who God says I am. Expose my enemies! Put them to shame and destroy their plans!

I will walk out of my season of hurt and pain and walk into a new season of justification and vindication!

It is in the omnipotent name of Jesus Christ, that I pray these prayers! Amen!

My Daily Prayer Journal

Prayer Plus Faith Equals Miracles

"Go, said Jesus, 'your faith has healed you.' Immediately he received his sight and followed Jesus along the road."

Mark 10:52

Almighty God who sits high and looks down low, move on my behalf today. Hear my prayers as spoken from the heart. The chastisement of my peace is upon You and I believe that just one touch from You can change a multitude of conditions. Today, open my mind and heart to the endless opportunities found in You!

I pray today for divine healing for myself and (or) for those connected to me. I cast down every manner of disease and affliction. I will be disease free; I will be free from all sickness! The spirit of infirmity has no place in my life! Your strength has graced me to make it through all adversities! O God, give me the stamina needed to continue this race of life.

Deliver me from my emotional and physical afflictions! I am free from infections, immune disorders, breast cancer, leukemia, pancreatic cancer, liver disease, heart disease, kidney disease, anxiety, stress, bipolarism, schizophrenia, depression and compulsive disorders. I will not expire before my time because of physiological diseases or psychological ailments. By Your stripes, I am healed and made whole.

I will walk in peace despite my circumstances. I am blessed beyond measure and there is no lack concerning me. Regardless of how fierce the winds blow, I will remain grounded in You, O God. I will build my hopes on nothing less than the promises of Your Word.

Even in the midst of the storm, Your grace sustains me. I can now sing songs of praise. What the enemy thought would be my demise has turned around for my good! No weapon formed against me shall prosper! The spirit of death will not take precedence over my life! I shall not die, but I shall live!

Increase my faith; when trouble comes, show me how to depend on my faith and to look only to You O God for answers to life's challenges.

You are Jehovah Rapha, the God that heals! By the blood of the lamb, I have overcome all sickness. I make this decree over my life: I will not lack in any area of my life for I am blessed physically, mentally and emotionally! I thank You in advance and declare these things to be so in the name of Jesus, Amen!

My Daily Prayer Journal

DAY
28

"I am the Lord, the God of all mankind. Is anything too hard for me?"

Jeremiah 32:27

Most gracious and loving Father, I thank You for being the Keeper of my soul! I thank You for Your mercy and grace! I honor You for the multitude of blessings bestowed upon me each and every day. I receive Your Word that declares that there is nothing impossible for God!

I now walk in the full liberty of Christ Jesus! Today, guide my every step; I pray for sensitivity to the voice of the Holy Spirit! I'm declaring a clear and focused mind! Help me to keep my mind stayed on You, for it is You O God that will keep me in perfect peace! My mind is renewed and has been released from oppression! I claim my deliverance from things and people that have kept me bound for far too long. If it's Your will O God, remove people and things that do me more harm than good!

I am victorious! I will see the salvation of the Lord! Your Word says that I am more than a conqueror through Christ Jesus! The enemy wants me to give up and walk away. I bind up the quitting spirit! I cast out the settling spirit! When giving up seems like it's the best thing to do, help me to look to Your strength to press through difficult moments.

In the midst of negative people and things around me, I hold firm to the plans You have for me. I declare that I will keep the faith! I will no longer walk in fear, but trust and believe that my future will be so much greater than my past! I wait with high levels of anticipation that all things concerning me are well!

What man thought was impossible, is now possible by Your power and Your might! Those things in my past that set out to destroy me did not consume me, but instead shaped me to walk into my purpose! The mistakes that I made in the past are far behind me. I realize that my trials and tribulations are only a testament of how You can turn negative situations around and use my pain for Your glory!

All things are working in my favor and for my good. So today, I choose to believe the report of the Lord! I will learn of You through my worship and through regularly studying Your Word; I stand boldly with the spirit of expectation to receive Your promises.

Through Christ Jesus, nothing is impossible! I pray these prayers and declare it to be so in the mighty, marvelous and matchless name of Christ Jesus! Amen!

My Daily Prayer Journal

DAY
29

"He performs wonders that cannot be fathomed, miracles that cannot be counted."

Job 5:9

You are Abba, my Father! You are beyond worthy to be praised! There are days when I get caught up with those things that negatively impact me and forget to give You thanks! There are times I neglect to recognize what a glorious day I have been blessed to see in You!

With all the hustle and bustle of life, I pray that I will not forget to express my gratitude for being able to experience life on earth, because it is truly a gift! Your love is expressed in a tangible way through the miracles You perform before me each day.

Today, I take this time to say thank You! Going forward, I will always reflect on the greatest Gift of all—Jesus Christ, our Savior! Help me to keep my mind stayed on You. You have done so many great things that are too marvelous for me to understand. Your ways are unsearchable and Your hand is untraceable! You perform countless miracles for me and those connected to me, time after time!

With You, O God all things are possible! I know that I can experience miracles in my life when I personally invite You in to intervene in my situation. You know what I have need of; meet every one of my needs. Today, O God come into every broken circumstance that has taken root in my life. Your Word reminds me that I do not have to settle for less than Gods best! I welcome Your presence into every negative issue or problem that I am facing.

There are moments when I have doubted and lacked in my own faith. Increase my faith today O God! I will walk by faith, and not by sight. Make Your purpose and plan for my life clear! If it is Your will, give me the faith to believe that You can and will perform those miracles that I desperately need and that which I hope for.

Even when I don't feel like my best, it is through Your strength that I can freely forgive those that have hurt or offended me. I repent for not walking in obedience to Your commandments and to Your Word. I pray now that all bondages of sin and evil be broken over my life. I cut every defiled thing off at the root: Unhealthy addictions, jealousy, greed, gossip, lying, anger, and negative words that others have been spoken over me and those connected to me. I refuse to focus on the negative but will meditate only on those things that edify You.

Even when it doesn't make sense, help me to lean and depend on You. Although my trust has been broken many times, I want to learn to trust You again one day at a time. It is through trusting and resting in You that I know You'll come to my rescue.

When unexpected circumstances arise, I pray this day that Your favor rest on me and that I begin to see the manifestation of miracles, signs, and wonders!

I ask these things in Jesus name, and decree that it shall come to pass in my life and in the life of those I love! Amen!

My Daily Prayer Journal

DAY
30

"For God so loved the world that he gave his one and only
Son, that whoever believes
in him shall not perish but have eternal life."

John 3:16

I will bless You O Lord at all times, and Your praises shall continually be in my mouth! Purge my heart by the power of Your Spirit! I believe and proclaim that there is power in prayer! Renew my mind through Your blood-washed Word.

I live to live again as I strive daily to gain eternal life! Thank You for Your gift of love. Thank You for dying on the cross for my sins. Thank You for loving me when I didn't love myself. It was Your unfailing love that lifted me out of bondage. So, I thank You for unconditional love that gives everlasting life with You! Ruin and destruction will no longer be my sustenance. I have been liberated to love others because You first loved me!

I realize that it is my responsibility to live right and to love others as you first loved me. My days of sorrow and heartache will be no more but will be replaced with the joy of You O Lord!

My past hurt shall not dictate my future. I refuse to allow my past hurt to defray me from loving others and keep me away from the love that I deserve. No longer will my past hurts dictate how I build future relationships.

Ecclesiastes 3 proclaims for everything there is a season and there is a time for every purpose under heaven. I walk in my season of now. Release me from those who have manipulated and controlled me as a result of prematurely opening my heart to the wrong individuals, in the wrong timing.

O God, help my heart to heal and to not wax cold as I walk into a new season in my life. Absolve me from all evil workers of iniquity. Hide me from the traps and ill intentions that satan seeks to implant within my heart.

I won't become a slave to bitterness, strife, envy, jealousy, and malice by allowing these things to control my actions. Help me to be slow to anger, but quick to love and forgive. Turn my heart from my own evil and wicked ways. I welcome God-filled and God-inspired love back into my heart. I will exercise self-control. Negative spirits have no power to control me!

Cause Your consuming fire to burn up everything that has inhabited my heart up until this point in time that are not pure and holy. Expand my understanding and open my mind to receive the knowledge and wisdom that You have imparted inside of me.

The glory of the Lord shall rise within me! My heart is already healed and made whole! I openly receive the love that I so deserve and refuse to become subject to settling for love that is unreal and not God-ordained. As I move forward by faith, refusing to look back; allow me to steal away in Your presence and receive all of You!

Let the words of my mouth and the meditations of my heart be acceptable unto You! I believe and decree this prayer to be so in Christ Jesus! And it is so! Amen!

My Daily Prayer Journal

DAY
31

"This, then, is how you should pray:"

Matthew 6:9-13

"Our Father in heaven, hallowed be your name, your

kingdom come, your will be done,

on earth as it is in heaven. Give us today our daily

bread. And forgive us our debts,

as we also have forgiven our debtors. And lead us

not into temptation,

but deliver us from the evil one."

My Daily Prayer Journal

"In our Gospel Jesus calls us to bear fruit as his disciples. If there is no fruitfulness in our lives, then God has to trim us and get us going in the right direction. Once we accept our fruitlessness and repent, God can move in our lives. A disciple of Jesus by nature bears fruit for the world. We need to look into our lives and see how we are affecting the world around us. We can only grow in our communion with the Lord if we are sharing him with others."

Fr. Gary Lauenstein, C.Ss.R.

Download the E-Book at
Amazon
Goodreads
Kobo
Smashwords

Email us to find out how to submit
video or written reviews:
RhemaWordPress@gmail.com

Audiobook Coming soon
January 2018

Upcoming Works from the Author

Guard Your Heart: Strategies to Kick the Enemy Out
of Your Life!